Save your family *& self* from viruses

Shiv Nandan

BlueRose Publishers

First Published in August 2020

ISBN:978-93-90380-60-2

BLUE ROSE PUBLISHERS

www.bluerosepublishers.com

info@bluerosepublishers.com

+91 8882 898 898

Cover Design:

Priyanshi Shukla

Typographic Design:

Ayushi Garg

Distributed by: BlueRose, Amazon, Flipkart, Shopclues

Dedication

This Book is dedicated to those who have suffered from viruses.

I am grateful to my friend Dr. Vipin Kapoor for guiding me in completing this work.

I am also indebted to Dr. Vishwas Virmani of Ortho Neuro Physiotherapy. Noida 201301, for helping to shoot the video and persuading me to take part in its completion.

This Book could not have been completed without the assistance from my daughters.

If this Book sails well, after the recovery of expenses and sustaining requirements, surplus revenue will be used to assist children of poor family's complete their education.

Corona virus has created havoc almost all over the world, though some countries especially in Europe and the Far East seem to have controlled it yet it can rear its head again for some reason or other like it happened in South Korea and this could happen in other parts of the world as well. It is still ravaging in some parts of the world and who can predict where it would all end.

Covid-19, officially known as SARS-2, is here to stay. It can affect anyone, anywhere, and those who are healthy will survive; the most vulnerable are the elderly and those with morbidities, such as diabetes, hypertension, asthma, persistent cough, high bad cholesterol levels, tuberculosis, cancer, or any other such problems. In fact, any weakness in the body could assist the growth and spread of Covid-19.

At present, dozens of organizations are working on producing vaccines; which of these will turn out to be effective, only time will tell. How many will perish during this time is anybody's guess. How many people would be able to get vaccinated and when? It will take a long time to vaccinate the entire world population, and it has to be repeated each year. Do repeated vaccination not become less effective? Would the side effects not take place? Mutation of this virus is expected to take place and there will have to be constant research and innovation, which could be expensive. It's a long struggle ahead.

There are probabilities that one could get affected by a person who is carrying the virus but it is in the initial stages and the symptoms have not yet reflected as they are mild and the carrier is not aware of them. It could be a barber, a chemist, a cab driver, a delivery person, a shopkeeper, a helper coming to work at home, or a mechanic who comes to repair something malfunctioning at home; it could be anybody. Spreading of the virus by sneezing is a major cause and it also spreads when the infected person talks and who so ever is in its vicinity of fewer than six feet is liable to get infected.

How long it will take for this virus to start receding in the countries it is spreading cannot be assumed and even if the spread is controlled all over the world it would not be its end. Most probably it will stay with humans forever and would probably, like influenza, raise its head now and then and especially in the winters.

More than half a million people die of respiratory diseases linked to influenza each year. Influenza viruses are constantly changing, with new strains appearing regularly and antibodies formed to fight a certain strain of 'flu virus' cannot help fight strains that are different immunologically.

There are three types of influenzas; A, B, and C. Type C causes 'flu' but symptoms are mild. There are potentially 198 different sub-type combinations of type A, but only 131 subtypes have been detected in nature and currently, A(H1N1) and A(H3N2), which changes more rapidly, circulate in nature. Type A is generally responsible for large flu epidemics. Type B is less severe but can be harmful and attacks humans only.Covid-19 can be described as the next generation, more aggressive and ferocious, if not deadly, cousin of influenza.

How many different types and combinations of Covit-19will evolve into is beyond anybody's guess. If influenza has 198 combinations, how many combinations of Covid-19 we would end up with. And how long it would take humans to understand and tame it well, there can be no assumptions; only time will tell. It is turning out to be more dangerous than assumed earlier, besides attacking the lungs, it can attack the kidneys, the brain, and the latest news is that it causes inflammation of the blood vessels which leads to the formation of blood clots which block blood vessels in the lungs and the heart leading to fatalities. It is a system-related disease, not just a virus, attacking the entire body.

To survive this scourge, humans need to develop immunity and overall health. Humankind has to prepare itself to confront and combat and not dodge it, as it is being done today, and neither fear it, as is happening at present. Is fear in the mind not one's enemy?

To combat any Covid-19it is essential to develop immunity, and the easiest way to do so is through the practice of yoga along with exercises like pushups and skipping, which can also be performed at home. And eat proper food. Yoga exercises suggested in this book are effective and most are easy to perform and these should take place without straining oneself. Each exercise has to be performed as per one's ability. A child of 6years age, or even less, can perform these yoga exercises eventually with ease. Children should not be forced to start with it; when they watch their parents they would get interested and it can begin as a fun sport, which can be encouraged by challenging them to show if they can perform. Slowly they will start enjoying it and take part, sometimes with some persuasion and cajoling, but some may need constant encouragement to perform.

However, do not force it on them when they are not well or have not slept well or on a certain day; if they just refuse to do it, it is better to let them be then. Be careful with the ones who often make excuses. Children should be made to understand that they have to develop immunity with exercise and proper diet and also take necessary precautions, or else, if Covid-19 strikes, it could be dangerous and could lead to the end of life. This understanding should lead to performance or else they will suffer and so will the parents.

A newborn baby can be exercised by folding its arms across the chest and gently pressing them on the chest and repeating this twice or thrice. Then folding their legs and pressing them gently against their body and repeating this twice or thrice. This should take place twice a day, once in the morning when they wake up and again in the evening when the stomach is empty. Even a baby just a few months old loves to be massaged, but it has to be done slowly and gently; this increases their appetite and they sleep better.

Don't ever stop them from crawling even when they are trying to crawl up the stairs, instead, encourage them to crawl, for example, by asking them to come to you. Better not to pick them up and put them in your lap; it is unhealthy and unhygienic. Babies do not grow in the lap. Never kiss a baby on its mouth or even the face – if youcannot resist, then kiss their feet or at the most kiss the neck, but hug them once in a while; a baby starts crying if left alone for too long, andthat's when they need a hug. Keep them in the cot when you cannot take care of them. Be sure it is deep enough and they cannotclimb out of it, as this will probably end in a fall. Babies love to listen to music, and when in their cot switch on the music; a happy baby will grow into a healthy baby.

As soon as a child learns to stand, it loves to walk and then run; don't stop them from walking or running, instead, encourage it, let them fall, and ignore it and they will try to stand on their own unless hurt and there is pain. Children between the age of 2 and 6 years and even elder to them should be made to run around the house. Get them involved in activities like pillow fighting, even wrestling or boxing, or any such activity which makes them exert themselves. Walking up and down the stairs is an option; such activities will increase their appetite and make them stronger, leading to living a happier life and beat Covid-19, if need be.

While the elderly can stay indoors and protect themselves, which in the long run may also prove harmful, children have to go out; is there any choice? Their childhood cannot be destroyed by keeping them at home. Besides, going to school they have to go out and play, meet friends, celebrate their birthdays, attend parties. You may stop them from visiting malls, but you cannot deprive them of an outing to have an ice cream or eat in a restaurant, attend family functions, and what about holidays? The only way out for them is to develop immunity and take necessary precautions and start living their normal lives without the fear of viruses.

Yoga is stretch exercises and in the beginning, the stretch should take place to the extent the body can perform without straining or pushing. Slowly and gradually, the body's stiffness starts to reduce, and stretching becomes easier and deeper, which leads to increased benefits. Yoga starts with exercising one's toes and ends with exercising the face muscles and even the eyes. The emphasis is on exercising internal organs, the parts which help build immunity, like the lungs, stomach, intestines, spine, heart, liver, veins/arteries, and above all, the brain.

Besides the internal organs, most other parts of the body get exercised as well, including the fingers, feet, legs, knees, thighs, hips, back, neck, shoulders, head, arms, joints; you name it. After each stretch there has to be a pause, for deep breathing to take place, while blood rushes through the now relaxed veins/arteries, washing them and an internal bath takes place, which is no less refreshing than an outer bath. This leads to increased fresh blood circulation, hence better metabolism and better appetite. Better digestion of food leads to better overall health and better immunity and one is all set to beat any viral or bacterial infection, including corona viral attacks

Yoga and the right food will keep morbidities like diabetes, hypertension, high bad blood cholesterol, and even cardio vascular attacks at bay and it slows down the aging process. These are not tall claims; the beneficial effects of yoga start showing within a few weeks if the practice is regular and proper. So get started and be ready to beat any infection, with the practice of Yoga along with your children and the elderly in the family, and start feeling good and confident without any fear in the mind.

Breathing deeply is a very important part of yoga and it is the breathing exercises, explained later (Nos. 6, 7 and 15) in this book, which strengthens the lungs. But we have a dangerous enemy and the lungs have to be strong for which exercises, which lead to breathlessness, like skipping and pushups are necessary. For how long one needs to or can skip will depend upon one's age, fitness level, and above all, the will.

There is no need to strain oneself, one can start with just a few skips and increase gradually to the required state for quick and deep breathing.

If elderly or overweight people are not able to skip, the best alternative, if possible, is to go for a brisk walk where the air is fresh, or walk up and down the stairs at home. The elderly have to be very careful walking up and down the stairs to avoid injury. In the beginning, clime slowly and carefully as many stairs easily possible and increase the number and speed gradually, yet carefully, and then climb as quickly as possible, to reach the state of some breathlessness, if possible. Take two breaks from this exercise in a week in the beginning and then reduce it to one if one can.

The young, instead of skipping, could run up the stairs but would have to start slowly first by climbing stairs quickly for a few days, and when one feels the legs have gained some strength then start running up. But before starting to run first warm up by walking up quickly and then run to a state of breathlessness. After running up the stairs, get to a place where the air is fresh for deep and quick breathing. Take a break once a week or two if necessary.

Another option, if possible, is to go for a run, after warming up, say by jogging, in the open and if possible run without covering your nose; if not, then at the end of the run get to an open place, preferably a garden, where there are no people around for about two meters and start breathing quickly and deeply, and then breathe slowly and deeply.

Yet another option, though not as good for those who are unable to skip such as the elderly or overweight people and small children, is the old type drill action, commonly known as Jumping Jack; jump open feet apart as much as is possible and comfortable, while simultaneously the arms go up to shoulder level, and quickly reverse the action without a break by bringing the feet back together with a jump and arms coming down to touch the thighs or get near them. Keep repeating this action until one reaches a state of breathlessness. Those who are not used to exercising or are overweight can start with just a few such actions and increase it slowly to as many as possible to a state-required to ensure deep and quick breathing.

Pushups (No.36) is another exercise to be undertaken, especially by men, not only to strengthen the lungs but also to develop some muscle mass required for an increase in basic strength to fight Covid-19 if need be. An attack could cause weakness in a person, similar to what happens when a severe attack of influenza takes place. Again, start slowly with just as many pushups as the body can take and increase it day by day with a break or two during the week to reach your optimum level. Young men and teenagers should get to 50 and take a break once or twice a week. The elderly can limit it to a minimum of three days a week and perform at the pace they find comfortable and to the number they find comfortable. No need to push yourself and neither ignore it.

Yoga along with pushups and running leads to increased testosterone levels and hence the increased desire to make love provided the intake of proper food takes place. These exercising efforts will not go waste even if or when the Covid-19 threat is over, which is unlikely. There will be long-lasting benefits for the rest of one's life. Good health is a basic requirement for a happy life.

Some ladies may find pushups difficult but should try and perform whatever the body can take, but be regular with yoga and skipping or the drill as Covid-19 will not spare anyone. Though there can be no alternative to pushups those who find it difficult to perform enough of them, a less effective alternative is, what could be described as sit-ups. Sit on a carpet, or a mat, or a hard bed stretch your legs in front and stretch your arms above the legs and lie down very slowly, don't drop, then try to sit up slowly. In the beginning, if need be, take the support of your elbow but give it up eventually. These can be performed any number of times as per one's ability and it's a way to control one's weight, especially around the waist. This exercise should be performed better twice a day about 10 times each, for 6 days a week.

Housewives, who work hard physically at home cooking, cleaning, dusting, need not skip or drill when not wanting to do so, but just thrice a week performance, along with yoga, will keep them young and healthy.

People who smoke and those who are overweight are in the danger zone as well. How to stop smoking and reduce weight is explained in the latter part of this book.

To reduce weight, besides proper diet the practice of yoga twice a day would be the first step, besides whatever other exercise is possible; the more the better. A yoga session in the morning will lift you and a session in the evening will remove fatigue and make you feel good.

An important factor that needs to be discussed is sleep, which has to be adequate for a healthy living. Grownups need a minimum of seven hours of good sleep in the summers, or 50 hours a week, and eight in the winters, or about 60 hours a week. Children and teenagers need more, while the elderly usually can do with less, but should be sleeping as much, if not more. Yoga and exercise help induce sleep and bedtime should take place at more or less the same hour at night. Sleeping at 11 pm and getting up at about 6 to 6.30 am, except on weekends, when sleeping late and getting up late takes place. But going to bed on Sunday at 11 pm, or earlier if weekend sleep has been inadequate, is essential, to be able to start the week freshly.

Those who are in the habit of sleeping late and getting up late and then rushing to work, and some without taking proper breakfast, are not living a healthy lifestyle. In the present way of life media plays an important part; it can be either a boon or a curse depending upon how it is used. Many people waste their time watching escapist programs, such as those full of violence, horror, revenge, torture, etc., which disturb the mind and hinder deep sleep. Even programs on the idiot box, such as serials based unrealistic stories are escapist and it is better to avoid them because they tend to leave you guessing, which can disturb sleep. It is better to watch programs with music, dance, or humor, which do not hamper sleep. Watching sports, wildlife, factual or history-based programs is good entertainment. But watching TV, using the cell or the computer has to be restricted to a certain period, including educational programs, for enough time for sleep and other important daily functions, such as quality time with family and friends when there is an opportunity.

Reading also induces sleep, though a novel can keep you awake, so it is better not to read a novel at bedtime. Read whatever you like, but poetry is best to read to induce sleep. Listening to soft music also induces sleep. The room one sleeps in should be dark and as quiet as possible; otherwise, cover your eyes with a dark cloth and insert cotton in the ears. A healthy body and a healthy mind complement each other and a mind that is deprived of sleep cannot be said to be healthy; sooner or later the negative effects will reflect. I cannot but mention an old idiom; "Early to bed, early to rise, makes a person healthy, wealthy and wise."

Research to fight Covid-19 has led to knowledge about specific vitamins and minerals required to combat this enemy, besides the normal basic requirement, which is as follows:-

Vitamins: C, D3 and B6, and Zinc.

All these can be acquired from food.

Vitamin C: Grapefruit, orange, lemon, Indian gooseberry, broccoli, cauliflower, tomato, kiwi, peppers, spinach, and other leafy vegetables.

Vitamin D3: Salmon, herrings, sardines, tuna, cod liver oil, egg yolk, mushrooms, exposure to the sun for an hour or more (preferably mid-morning).

Vitamin B6: Eggs, meat, poultry, soya beans, bread, peanuts, boiled potatoes, bananas, and melon seeds.

Zinc: Meat, chickpeas, dried figs, lentils, beans, nuts, whole grains, and watermelon.

Seeds are wonder foods, their value remains unrealized and several are just wasted, the following information may change attitudes.

Pumpkin seeds: High in magnesium, antioxidants, improves prostate and bladder health, high in fiber assists blood sugar level.

Melon seeds: Rich source of proteins, vitamin B6, thiamine, niacin, magnesium, copper, zinc, potassium, and phosphorous.

Chia seeds: Good source of fiber, protein, Omega 3s, magnesium, phosphorus, zinc, vitamins B3, B1, B2.

Hemp seeds: Rich source of protein, fiber, Omega 3s and 6s, antioxidant healthy for heart, skin, and joints.

Watermelon seeds; Also a rich source of proteins, Omega 3 and Omega 6 fatty acids, magnesium, zinc, copper, potassium, and vitamins. Watermelon seeds should be taken in moderation, owing to side effects.

Fiber: Normalizes bowel movement, decreases chances of constipation, and lowers cholesterol levels, which may reduce blood pressure and sugar level. It aids in maintaining a healthy weight and increases life expectancy. One must not allow oneself to get constipated, as it can lead to other problems. For overall health, one should clear the stomach and throw out toxins once every 24 hours. Those who are unable to do this should take some hot milk, an hour before going to bed. And walk in the 8 formations to digest it.

Diet, as we all know, is a very important factor for good health; though there is plenty of awareness in this regard, detailed suggestions have been made in the latter part of this book and there will be no harm in repeating certain important factors here, especially about the diet of children.

Probably the healthiest food on earth is the humble egg, nature's multivitamin/mineral product. It contains an amazing range of nutrients and is loaded with vitamins, minerals, high-quality protein, and various other lesser-known nutrients. Each egg contains B12, B2, A, B5, and E, as well as small amounts of almost every other vitamin required by humans, and selenium. It also contains minerals, such as calcium, iron, potassium, zinc, manganese, and more.

It should be known that almost all nutrients are contained in the yolk; the white contains only protein but no fat.

People are under the impression that eggs raise bad cholesterol levels, but studies have shown that eggs improve the cholesterol profile; they raise HDL (good) cholesterol and increase the size of LDL particles, which should lower the risk of heart disease. Those in doubt should consult their doctor.

The fact remains that with yoga and exercise and the resulting improved digestive system, the digestion of eggs would be easy and would prove to be the best food to take.

A word for vegetarian and vegan friends, eggs on the table have no life; those containing lives are separated for hatching, and this is another great aspect of nature concerning eggs. Is there any flesh in the egg on the table? But the vegetables we eat and the plants they grow with have life, don't they? Talk to plants and they grow; one person in the UK talked to his pumpkin grown at home and it grew up to weight 40kg and he was awarded for the same in an exhibition there. Talk to an egg and see if it will grow. Educated vegetarians should look at this with an open mind; is there any other food that can provide the same nutrition as an egg? If they are unable to eat eggs they should encourage their children to take eggs, as there is no other food which can provide such nutrition, and giving them substitutes is not warranted.

Proper food should take care of the required nutrition, for solid immunity, along with Yoga, with some medication when necessary.

For breakfast, start with some apple and an orange, and, depending on the child's age, they should be given one or two eggs almost daily, either half-boiled, three quarters boiled, or full boiled whichever they like, with salt and lemon. For a change, children can also be given fried eggs or scrambled eggs prepared in butter. Other preparation methods may destroy some of their food value but would be fine over the weekend.

The next food to be given to them should be a bowl of porridge oats prepared in milk but no sugar, instead add some banana or some other sweet fruit like mango for change. Also add some nuts like almonds and walnuts, with some dried sweet berries or raisins, preferably black, and chickpeas. How much the child caneat will depend on the child's age and its appetite.

The other good breakfast food for a change is muesli with milk and added nuts, as the muesli available in the market does not contain enough of them. Add some banana or some other fruit as per the child's desire. Dried figs contain zinc and, if possible, should be part of breakfast or given as a snack. If there is an appetite, add a few dates.

Children tend to gulp food, especially when hungry or in a hurry, and this should be controlled. Food must be chewed well, and the habit has to be formed as a child. We have all the time in the world for other things, but eating food, the life-giving force rarely gets the time it deserves.

Grown-up or healthier children, especially teenagers, may need more than what has been suggested, in which case a slice of brown bread with some cheese can be a choice, or whatever else they prefer. None should remain hungry, but don't let them overeat either, which will be counterproductive. No child should be overweight, as it would be difficult, if not dangerous if Covid-19 strikes.

A hot beverage is necessary after breakfast, and milk is the best choice for children.

A traditional drink which would require some time to prepare is suggested for all to be taken during winters for at least a month. Boil a spoonful of shredded ginger along with two cloves and some cinnamon and licorice root in more than two glass of water until it reduces to one. Then add about half a teaspoon of turmeric powder and one-third of a teaspoon of black pepper. Let it brew for about two minutes, then add some lemon and honey to taste and let all, including children, the elderly, and especially those who have any type of problem with their respiratory system and the throat, take it.

This traditional mixture is supposed to build immunity and its benefits have been known for centuries. These products have been used for ages in herbal medicines and the claims are not fictitious. The benefits of ginger and turmeric are described in the latter part of this book and the other products have known to have benefits as follows:

Cloves: High in antioxidants. Contain important nutrients. May, kill bacteria. May improve liver and bone health. May, reduce stomach ulcers.

Cinnamon: Loaded with antioxidants. Have anti-inflammatory properties and has an anti-diabetic effect.

Licorice Root: Soothes stomach and throat pain, known to improve the respiratory system, reduces stress, and protects skin and teeth.

This drink has been administered to people suffering from cough or asthma since long before the discovery of modern medication because it strengthens the respiratory system, the object of the Covid-19 attack.

Proteins, carbohydrates, vitamins, and some unsaturated fat is necessary for healthy living, and detailed suggestions are given in the latter part of the book, but certain further suggestions about children's diet are warranted. Children should not be allowed to eat unhealthy snacks, like Potato Chips and other deep-fried snacks, which are fried in saturated fats and contain extra salt; they kill appetite and are the worst type of snacks to take.

Instead, the best snacks for children are fresh fruits, seeds, and vegetables, such as a carrot, lettuce leaves, cucumber, and tomato, which is a fruit and biting it is more delicious than cutting it open before eating it. If parents eat these vegetables the children will also eat them. The other good snacks children can have are dried apricots, and chickpeas, besides dry figs and dates if not already taken enough during breakfast.

Occasionally, give them cookies or biscuits, preferably made from products like sorghum, pearl millet, rye flakes, or barley. Chocolates can be given as a snack, but not the ones with a lot of sugar content. Black chocolate with nuts is a good choice.

When thirsty, give them a glass of milk or milkshake especially after sports or exercise, or a glass of juice, fresh if possible, lemonade or just plain water, but avoid colas as much as possible, better none at all.

Other foods to be avoided are the ones made from refined white flour-like noodles, pasts, macaroni, etc. Its excess carbohydrate content is believed to be cancerous. Also, avoid foods with high salt and sugar content.

Parents know what else to feed the children with, to make a balanced diet, but usually not enough vegetables are fed to the children. School-going children have limited choices for lunch and for most of them, it is a sandwich; some good choices are cheese, cucumber, and tomato or an egg, especially for a teenager, in brown bread. With an apple, or a pear or whichever fruit the child prefers. Give them a pack of juice they like, or milkshake, or if possible a yogurt-based drink; a shake made from yogurt and water with some salt is good to take.

To ensure the required intake of vegetables takes place, abowl of salad with ingredients as suggested in the latter part of this Book should also be served to children before other food is served. But provide them the dressing they like so that they eat the salad for sure.

Besides salads, cooked vegetables must also be served; the darker the color of the vegetables, the more the value. Leafy green vegetables, beetroot, eggplant, and cabbage should be part of the diet as often as possible.

Protein in the west comes mainly from meat, poultry, fish, or seafood, but another good source of cheaper protein is lentils and beans. Lentils are an excellent source of B vitamins, iron, magnesium; potassium, and zinc, besides fiber, and beans to contain iron, potassium, and magnesium, as well as folate and fiber. These are underrated foods in the west and should be part of the diet not only for the children but also for everyone else. It would add to the variety and taste of food and at a lower cost. Parents should learn how to cook lentils, beans, and vegetables the way Indians do, and it is possible to do so without making it spicy, though a bit of spice adds to taste and many are good, such as black pepper, which is good for the gut and probably the brain. Once children acquire the taste, they love it and it would add variety to their meals. Lentils also help develop immunity.

The best dessert is fruits, such as mangoes, melon, watermelon, pears, plums, and the like. These help to clear the stomach in the morning and throw out toxins, a good habit to form by all.

Foods known to assist develop immunity are:-

Citrus fruits: Grapefruits, oranges, tangerines, lemon, limes, and Indian Gooseberries. Papaya, Apples, Garlic, Ginger, Turmeric, Flax Seeds, Yogurt, Red Bell Peppers, Broccoli, Spinach, Kale, Cabbage, Beets, Eggplant, Almonds, Figs, Walnuts, Chickpeas, Salmon, Poultry, Eggs, Sardines, lintels, Red Kidney Beans, Green Tea

Regular balanced consumption of these foods will lead to better immunity along with exercise.

Garlic a top wonder food, which contains almost all ingredients required by the human body, if it cannot be taken with salads, a clove or two of it could be cut and swallowed with water after food, proportion as per age and built.

Other than exercise and diet, the next most important requirement is hygiene; unhygienic conditions are a cause of many problems in life, and even more so than normal, with Covid-19.Besides the maintenance of normal hygiene practices, frequent washing of hands with soap is known to all as protection, because soap kills most viruses. Brushing of the teeth twice a day is essential, besides gargling with salt water once a day by all and for the elderly twice a day would be better. Don't share personal items. Avoid eating and drinking in public places. Wash fresh groceries well.

Besides sneezing, talking is a major cause of transmission of this infection; hence the face and the mouth should be well covered when visiting places with people around. A minimum distance of a meter or more if possible must be maintained under all circumstances. As a further precaution, it would be better to talk or listen as least as possible and spend the least possible time in any crowded place.

But it is not right to keep your mouth covered when it is not necessary, such as while traveling in the car, when at home, or walking when nobody is in the vicinity for a meter and a half. It is harmful to keep the mouth and nose covered for too long, as one repeatedly is rebreathing the bad breath exhaled from your lungs, which has to be thrown outand fresh air inhaled.

Whenever there is an opportunity when nobody is in the vicinity and there is open space around, then remove the mask from the nose and breathe in and out for as long as possible and convenient. It's better to change the mask after 4 hours if used continuously, for which it may be necessary to carry an extra mask when leaving the house or an extra handkerchief, which can be washed for re use.

All these precautions are necessary, but what is most important is building up immunity. Children have to go to school or college; all have to go to work and start living a normal life. Going shopping, meeting friends, eating in a restaurant, going for a holiday – and why not? A fear psychosis has been created, and it has to be overcome, for the world to start functioning as it should. Offices have to start functioning properly, manufacturing has to get started again, trade has to be restored, shops, markets, and malls have to open, services have to be restored and travel and transport have to resume.

The entire world can be on its feet if the fear of corona in the mind is got rid of. The way to do this is to build immunity, and basic immunity can be achieved within about twenty days. Then let it strike if it has to and the one with immunity will be through with it, with proper medication in a few days like an attack of influenza.

It is assumed that a very large section, some estimate it to be 70% of the world population, will probably have to go through it sooner or later. Though this is an unlikely probability should the world not be prepared for it?

With continuous advances in medication, unless the case is severe, patients will start getting treated at home, But will need isolation in a separate room with a healthy member of the family, with guidance from a doctor, taking care of the patient, and with all the necessary precautions. And one would be able to overcome it like an attack of influenza if healthy.

Would corona virus ever vanish it may be controlled by one way or the other but would rear its head in different forms. Hence, developing immunity is the answer. Besides, this preparation will help live a better life, with or without the epidemic, and leave humanity prepared for the next such attacks from nature which could continue to take place and the next virus could be worse than the present one, probably to keep humans on their toes.

All said and done, regular practice of Yoga and the suggested exercise, with proper diet and proper hygiene, will strengthen the immune system to the extent required. And in case, for whatever reason, the pandemic subsides, which is unlikely, and people stop suffering from it, the immunity built and the state of health achieved will lead to happy living for the rest of one's life. It's a win-win situation.

The suggested yoga exercises known as Asana have been selected for their effect and ease of performance, some may be a bit difficult to perform in the beginning but eventually, when the body stiffness is reduced, these can also be performed with ease. Many people find it difficult to leave the bed in the morning and time can be saved if the moment one wakes up could start with yoga exercises as described. It is advisable to take a bath before getting into bed as one sleeps better and the body is less stiff in the morning.

As soon as you wake up, lie flat on your back, without the pillow, your hands at your sides. The mind and body ought to be relaxed owing to proper sleep. Don't let your mind start wandering, don't let any disturbing thought enter your mind, keep it silent. In the morning, this is not difficult because the mind is already rested and calm, especially if the sleep has been deep. To control the mind from wandering, concentrate on the exercises.

Breathe normally.

1. Start with moving your toes by bending them backwards and forward for a while.
2. Stretch one foot away from the body and the other towards the body; hold for a second or two, then stretch them in the opposite direction, repeat at least thrice, or more if you wish.
3. Rotate the feet clockwise thrice and then rotate them anti clockwise thrice or more if you want to.
4. Press your knees down towards the ground few times.
5. Next, fold your left knee and bring the foot towards your bottom and then straighten the leg. Repeat this at least thrice. Repeat the same action with your right leg.

Now, you are ready to spring out of your bed. Keep a thermos of hot water, especially in the winters, next to your bed and have two glass of water. The bacterium in the mouth, when taken in have a similar reaction as a vaccine and is traditionally known to be beneficial, it is not harmful for sure, and use will prove this. In case it does not seem appropriate, then clean your mouth and have two glass of water. Drinking water in the morning has several benefits; it hydrates the body and helps the clearing of the stomach. Use the toilet and walk out to open space.

If open space or a balcony is not available in the house, then stand at an open window with cross ventilation, if possible, for deep breathing.

Deep breathing of fresh air is an important aspect of yoga; it relaxes the mind and helps to throw out toxic heavy air which settles at the bottom of the lungs, which we keep accumulated during the day and sleep with at night. With deep breathing, you are providing the lungs with fresh air which purifies blood better for the brain and the body. 70% of this purified blood goes to the brain, which runs the body and 30% to other parts. Purer the blood better is the immune system.

6. A. Stand erect, face and mind relaxed, head straight, heels and feet apart as comfortable, arms by the sides, inhale quickly through nostrils and exhale deeply and quickly through the mouth at least thrice.

   B. Then inhale and exhale quickly through the nostrils only and keep doing so, if comfortable, for about half a minute, or less.

7. Even with these steps, heavy air is left at the bottom of the lungs, which should be thrown out and replaced with fresh air.

A. Stand erect, press your right nostril, with your right thumb, and inhale the fresh air slowly and deeply through your left nostril.

B. When the lungs are completely filled up, press your left nostril firmly with the right forefinger so that the nose is completely blocked.

C. Hold the breath for at least half the time taken or even more to fill the lungs. In the beginning, it could be less. This duration should be constant. This allows the fresh air to mix with the toxic air at the bottom of the lungs before it is thrown out.

D. Lift the thumb from the right nostril, while the left nostril is still closed firmly with the right forefinger, and then slowly breathe out completely through the right nostril. Note you are breathing in from the left nostril and breathing out from the right nostril.

E. As soon as you have exhaled through the right nostril, hold the breath out for a second or two then begin to inhale from the right nostril itself while the left nostril remains pressed with the right-hand forefinger. Fill the lungs by breathing steadily and deeply and when the chest is filled absolutely, press the right nostril with your right thumb firmly so that no air can leak out and hold for as long as comfortable.

F. Then lift the right forefinger from the left nostril and start exhaling slowly and steadily and blow the air out of the lungs completely. Repeat the entire act from A to F thrice so that no toxic air is left in the lungs. Now, you will feel certain calmness in the mind and certain freshness in the brain, if there is any.

This exercise is known as "Pranayam" and is one of the most beneficial of all yoga exercises because its performance leads to maximum purification of the blood, which leads to better health. If it is performed in an open space, such as a garden or where the air is fresh and oxygen content is high, such as in the mountains, one can feel not only the freshness in the brain but a unique feeling of being healthy and calm.It's a wonderful feeling.

One circle of Pranayam implies breathing in from, say, the right nostril and breathing out from the left nostril then breathing in from the left nostril and breathing out from the right nostril.

Deep breathing is necessary after every Assan not only to allow the blood to become better purified but also because the pause leads to blood rushing through the relaxed arteries and veins after stretching and hence washing them; a kind of internal bath takes place.

Pranayam can also be performed while sitting or lying down and could be performed after any Asana, which is a bit strenuous or takes more time. But there is no need to hold the breath, just inhale deeply from one nostril and exhale from the other. It is your decision whether to just inhale and exhale deeply to normalize breathing or perform Pranayam after an Asana.

Do not allow the mind to wander during this period; instead, keep it silent and concentrate on the exercise. There is a tendency to stop breathing during a performance, which should not happen. Non-stop breathing has to continue during exercise, so please bear this in mind, as the stoppage of breathing during the exercises is unhealthy.

This is what science has to say about blood circulation and the value of deep breathing of fresh air is obvious:

"From the time of birth till death the heart works continuously. Every day the heart pumps 7000 liters of blood, of which 70% is pumped to the Brain and the remaining 30% to the rest of the body.

How does the heart work so efficiently and effectively? Because, it follows a discipline. In a normal condition, the heart takes 0.3 seconds to contract (systole) 0.5 secs to relax (diastole). Therefore, 0.3 + 0.5 secs are required by the heart to complete one beat (1 cardiac circle). That means, in 1 minute the heartbeats 72 times, which is considered a normal heartbeat.

During the relaxing phase of 0.5 secs, the impure blood travels through the lungs and, if the lungs are healthy, it becomes 100% pure.

In some stressful conditions, the body demands more blood in less time, and in this situation, the heart reduces the relaxing period of 0.5 secs to 0.4 secs. Thus, in this case, the heartbeats 82 times in one minute and only 80% of the blood gets purified, on more and more demand, the relaxing time reduces to 0.3 secs and then only 60% of blood gets purified.

Imagine the consequences of the less oxygenated blood circulating in our brain and arteries. Deep breathing of fresh air is the key to ensure better-oxygenated blood circulation in our brain and arteries, a very important factor for a healthy and long life.

Factors responsible for the activity of the brain:-

1. 25% to 30% is due to the diet we consume
2. 70% to 75% is due to emotions, attitudes, memories, and other processes of the brain.

8. A. Stand erect, face and mind relaxed, keep breathing normally, bring your chin down to touch the chest and hold for a while. Then stretch your head backward as far as possible and hold and then straighten it. Repeat this twice or thrice.

   B. Again bring the chin near to the chest and then rotate your face and the chin up towards the right shoulder. Hold for a while and rotate it back slowly towards the left shoulder; hold for a while and bring it back to the center and straighten the head. Inhale and exhale deeply. Repeat twice.

   C. Standing erect, turn your straight head towards the right shoulder and bring the chin as near as possible to the right shoulder and hold for a while. Then straighten it and repeat this act towards the left shoulder, hold for a while and bring it back, inhale and exhale deeply. Repeat twice or thrice.

   D. Standing erect, bend your neck towards the right shoulder, hold for a while, then straighten it and bend it towards the left shoulder. Hold for a while and then straighten it, inhale and exhale. Repeat twice or thrice.

   E. Standing erect, hold your hands behind your back and then bend your neck and waist slightly backward and pull your hands down as far as possible. Hold for a while and then release and repeat twice, then normalize breathing. People of middle age who spend a lot of time at a desk should repeat all these 5 steps at least thrice. And for better results repeat these exercises at about 4 pm or before going to bed.

F. Standing erect, raise your arms to your shoulder level and then swing your arms towards the left and backward as far as possible. The torso twists towards the left and the face also should turn towards the left with eyes looking at the left hand, hold for a while, and then swing towards the right completely as the face also turns right, looking at the right hand. After holding for a while swinging toward the left again, hold for a while and swing back towards the right. Hold for a while and then bring the arms in front and lower them down, then inhale and exhale to normalize breathing.

9. A. Stand erect, keep your feet hip-width apart, then raise your arms above your head and join palms, so that the upper arms are next to your ears. Then

slowly curve your upper body backward along with the arms and the head until the waist also curves backward, as far as is comfortable.

B. Keep breathing and hold in this curved posture for about 5 seconds, or as long as is comfortable. Then slowly straighten yourself in reverse and repeat this activity once or twice. Standing erect, perform Pranayam.

10. A. Stand erect, feet hip-width apart. Raise your arms above your head and join palms. Inhale and while exhaling, bend your knees until the straight body comes down about 6" and stay in this posture as if sitting on a chair, hold for a while keep breathing. Then slowly straighten your knees up, inhale and exhale and repeat the act.

Those suffering from pain in the knees avoid this exercise.

B. Stand erect, raise your arms to shoulder level and bring them in front, lift your heel up along with the body; hold for a while and then bring it down and lift again and repeat this another three times or more.

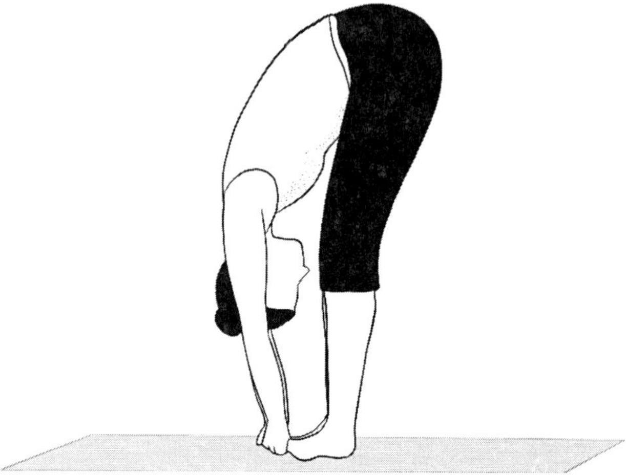

11. A. Standing erect, raise your arms up, palms facing front, inhale deeply and while exhaling, bring the hands down slowly towards your feet and try to hold your toes or get as near as possible and hold in this bent position for a comfortable while. Knees should not bend, keep breathing.

B. Then grasp the lower part of your legs by your hand from behind and bring your head as close as possible to the straight knees. Hold for a comfortable while and return slowly to the standing posture. Inhale and exhale slowly and deeply, to normalize breathing.

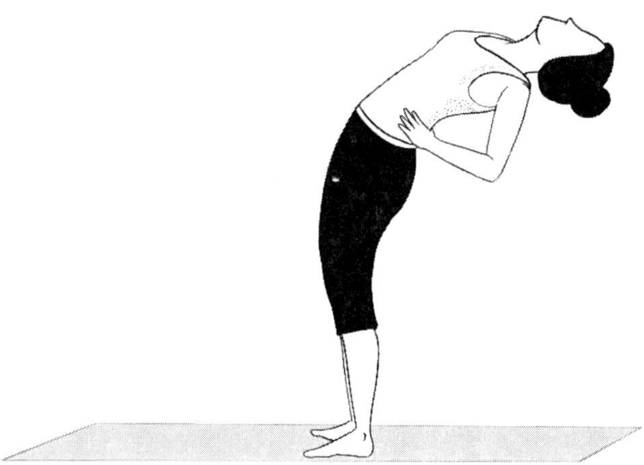

12. Stand erect with heels about 6 inches apart, or as comfortable, then keep your hands on the waist and bend your torso backward as far as is comfortable, hold for a comfortable while and then slowly straighten the torso. Inhale and exhale or perform Pranayam to normalize breathing. Repeat No.11 and then No.12 once or twice.

13. A. Standing erect, with heels and feet together, lift your right arm up, take a deep breath and, while exhaling, bend at the waist towards the left with the left arm stretching towards your left foot, right arm curved over the head and around it with fingers pointing towards the ground; keep breathing. The body should not bend forwards or backward but should remain straight. Hold for a

comfortable while and then slowly return to standing erect, inhale, and exhale.

B. Repeat the same action by bending towards the right side and the left arm going around the head above it. Inhale and exhale and normalize breathing. Repeat the Asana on both sides twice. After completion, normalize breathing. If need be perform Pranayam.

14. A. Standing erect, mind, and face calm, jump and move the feet apart so that the heels are about two or more feet apart, depending upon your height and the length of your legs. Bend forward and when the torso is parallel to the ground, bring your right hand towards your left foot and touch the right hands back to the outer side of the left

leg, or get the right hand as near as possible to the left foot and hold.

B. Now raise the left hand up and turn your face up to look at the fingers of the left hand. Hold for a comfortable while.

C. Now bring your left hand towards the right foot and touch the backside of the hand on the outer side of the right leg, or get the hand as near as possible to the right foot, while the right-hand goes up and the face is turned upwards to look at the stretched above right hand. Hold for a while and keep breathing. Repeat the entire act twice or more.

D. Put your hands on the waist and jump to bring the feet nearer, slowly straighten your torso and stand erect and perform Pranayam.

15. Please ensure that the next step is undertaken with care and there is no hurry about it. It must be done slowly and steadily,

A. Standing erect, face and mind relaxed, feet a few inches apart, inhale slowly, steadily and deeply through the nostrils, hold for a while and then exhale slowly, steadily, and completely in a manner so that no air is left in the lungs or the stomach.

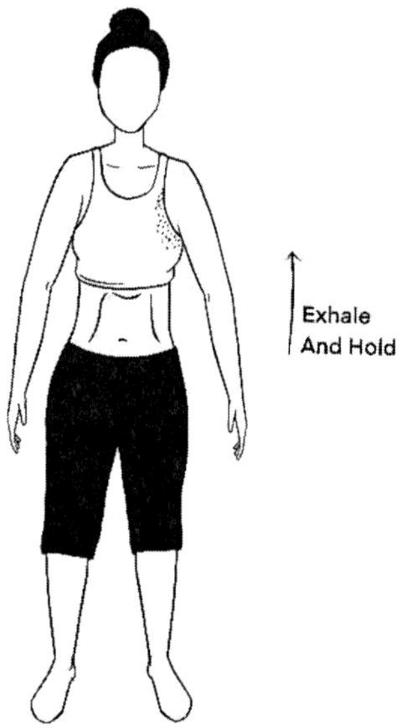

B. Then pull the entire abdomen area towards the spine and hold the completely pulled-in stomach and hold your breath, as long as possible and comfortable. With time, this period of holding the breath should increase up to a minute especially by the young and the healthy. This leads to the lungs getting used to surviving without air and is a weapon against the corona virus. When it cannot be held any longer, then start inhaling very slowly and steadily until the lungs are filled with air. Normalize breathing and repeat the Asana.

C. Standing erect fill your lungs absolutely and push your stomach out as much as possible, hold your breath and stay in this posture as long as and then exhale slowly.

Drink a three-fourth glass of water and lie down on a mat or a carpet, preferably in the open, otherwise in a balcony. If not possible, then lie in the part of the house where there is cross ventilation. The last choice could be your bed, provided it is not soft and the windows of the room are open for fresh air circulation. Lie across it in the middle completely relaxed, as if you were a dead person. Keep the arms by your sides, let the feet fall naturally open, and silence the mind. Let the mind check that there is no stress in any part of the body, starting with the feet then the legs, knees, thigh, stomach, back, chest, arms, shoulders, neck, and face.During this check, slow and deep breathing should continue and your mind should remain absolutely calm and not wander.

16. Lying on your back, join your heels and the feet, stretch your arms out to the side, 90 degrees to the body, inhale and while exhaling, raise your right leg straight up 90 degrees to the ground, hold for a few seconds and bring it down slowly. Repeat with the left leg. Inhale and exhale and repeat the exercise once again. Inhale and exhale slowly and deeply to normalize breathing. Those with pain in the hip should repeat this Asana several times as required.

17. A. Lying down, bring the arms to your side and raise the right leg 90 degrees, then raise your chest and hold the right leg with both hands as high as possible and bring your head towards the knee, keep the leg straight. Hold for a comfortable while and return to lying down. Normalize breathing.

B. Repeat the same with the other leg.

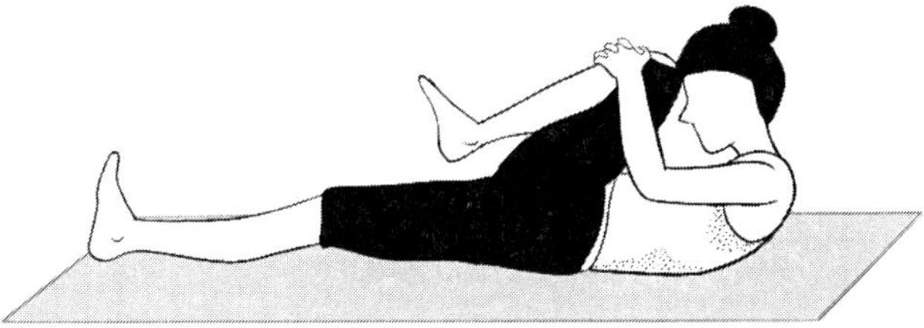

18. A. Lying down, fold your left knee and bring it near your chest and then grasp the leg below the knee with your hands and pull it towards your chest, then lift your head and touch it with the knee. Hold for a while and then release slowly and straighten the leg, inhale and exhale deeply and repeat with the right leg.

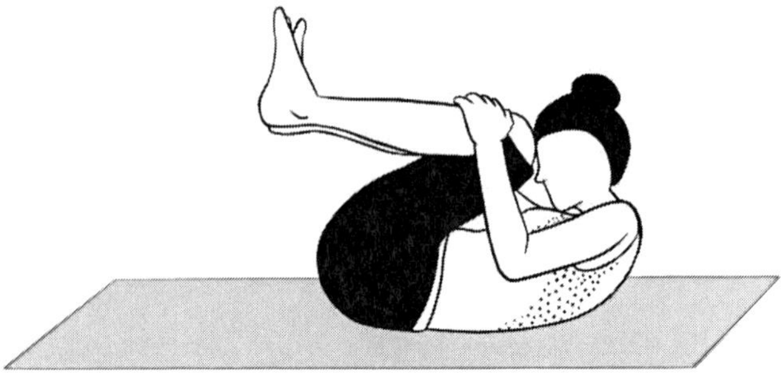

B. Fold both the knees and bring them towards your chest, then clasp your legs below the knees with your hand and raise your head to touch the knees. Hold for a comfortable while. Remove the hands from the legs and slowly stretch your legs straight, keep breathing, while bringing the head back to the ground.

C. Inhale and exhale and repeat the entire exercise once or twice and normalize breathing.

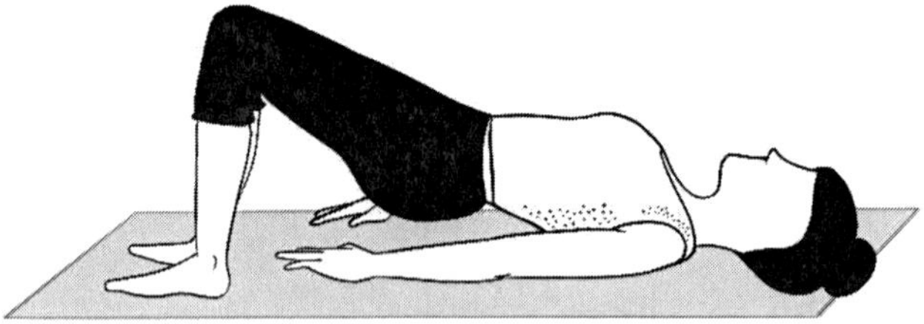

19. Lying down, fold your knees and place your feet on the ground about 4-5 inches away from your bottom and about 4-5 inches apart, arms by the sides and palms touching the ground. Then lift the tail bone-about 2-3 inches above the ground and hold for a comfortable while. Then bring the lifted part slowly to rest on the

ground and straighten the legs. People who suffer from tailbone pain should repeat this Asana as required.

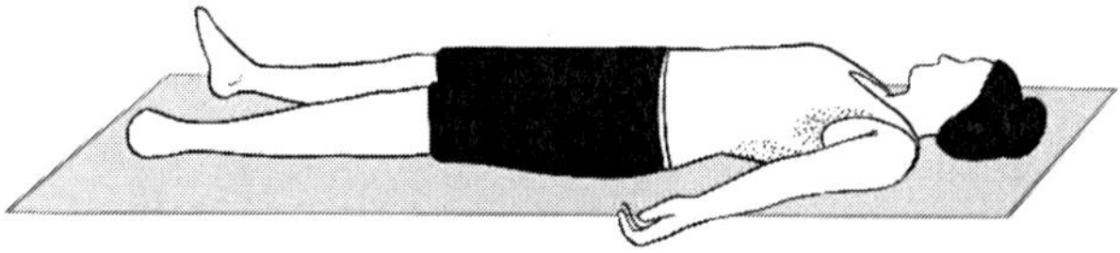

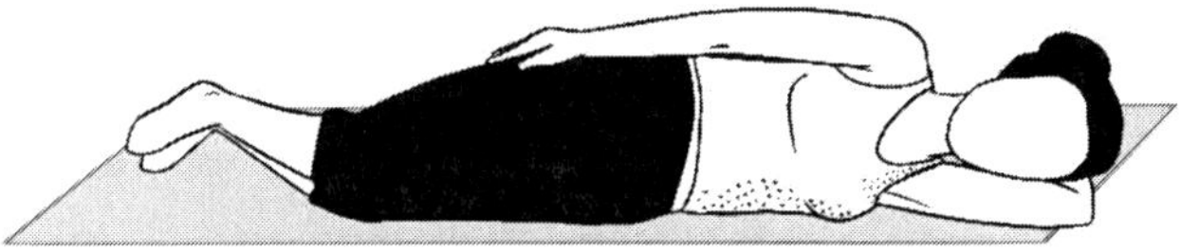

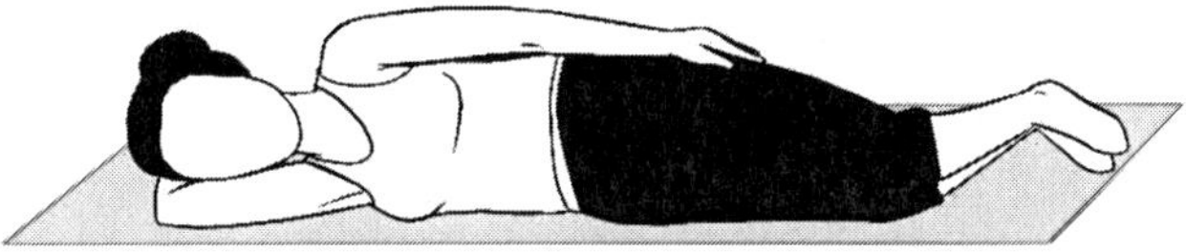

20. Shav Asana. There are certain Asana which are a bit difficult to perform and take some extra time and longer breathing is required for which an Asana known as Shav Asana should be performed, which is as follows:-

    Lying on the back, Inhale slowly and deeply and exhale slowing and repeat twice; when exhaling for the third time turn your body to the right, fold your legs about 45 degrees and bring your right arm under your head. Then inhale deeply and, while exhaling, turn your body to lie on your back. Inhale and exhale deeply once or twice and repeat the Asana on the other side. This Asana should be performed after every difficult Asana, not only to normalize breathing but also to allow the blood to rush through the arteries/veins washing them.

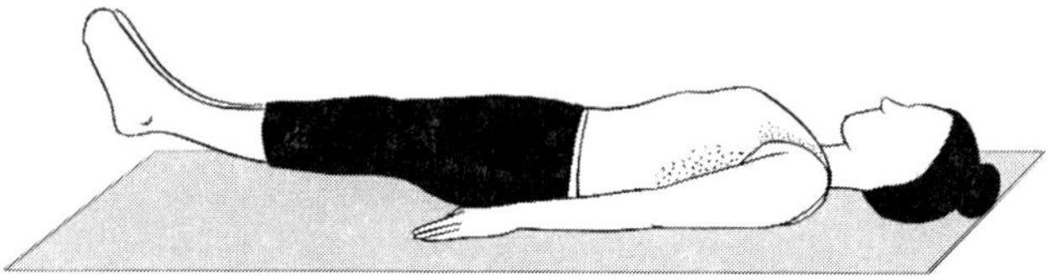

21. A. Join the feet, place the palms of your hands flat on the ground by your sides, then raise your feet about three inches above the ground and hold for a comfortable while; keep breathing and then lower the feet slowly. Inhale and exhale deeply.

B. Lying down straight, inhale and while exhaling, raise your straightened and joined legs up slowly, taking support from the palms/arms, if necessary. Keep raising the straight, joined legs slowly and bring them 90 degrees to the body and hold for a comfortable while. Palms on the ground, bring the legs down very slowly, never drop them, and ensure breathing does not stop. When back to lying perform the breathing Asana No. 20, known as Shav Asana, described above, to normalize breathing. Repeat the Asana once or twice.

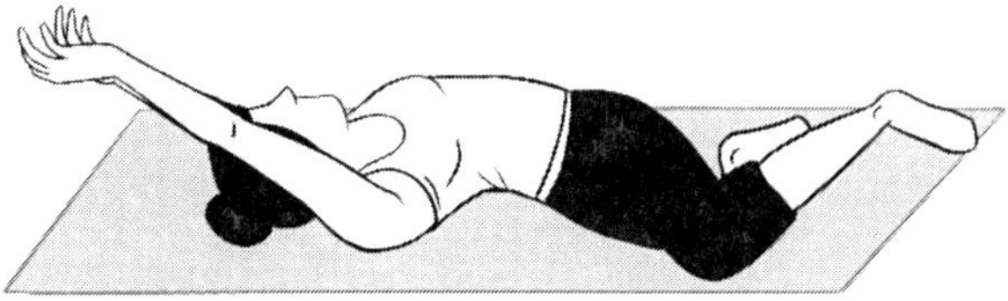

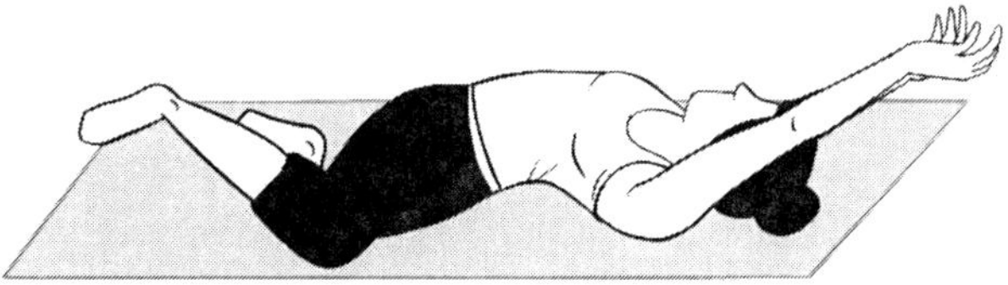

22. Lying on your back, bring your feet towards your bottom and then bend your knees towards the right so that the right leg and knee touch the ground and the left leg rests on the right leg firmly, while the arms get stretched towards the left beyond the head and the face turned to look at the hands. Hold for about 5 seconds and then slowly return to lying down straight. Then bend the legs towards the left and stretch the arms towards the right and the face turned to look at the hands. After holding for about 5 seconds, release and straighten the body. Inhale and exhale and repeat the entire Assan at least once. If necessary perform Pranayam to normalize breathing.

23. A. Lying down, raise your straightened, and joined legs up slowly by 90 degrees. Press the palms on the ground and carry the feet towards the back of your head, while the spine gets curved, and try to bring your feet down to touch the ground behind the head. If not possible in the beginning then hold the feet as near as possible to the ground. Sustain this posture as long as is comfortable. Meanwhile, arms and the palms remain touching the ground.

B. Then slowly reverse the procedure keep breathing straighten the legs and bring your legs down slowly, be sure the legs don't drop, and normalize breathing by performing Shav Assan No. 20 while lying down. Repeat if you wish.

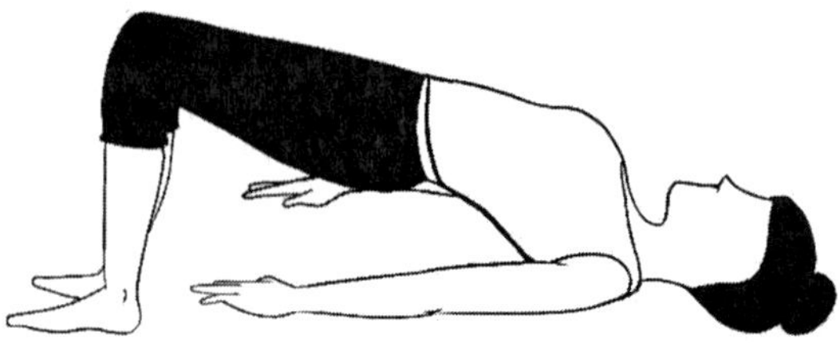

24. Fold your knees and place your feet about 4-5 inches away from your bottom and about 4-5 inches apart,

hands by your sides, palms on the ground, then lift the hips up as much as possible and comfortable and shoulders remain touching the ground, hold for at least 5 seconds or more. Then bring the lifted part slowly to rest on the ground. Normalize breathing. Repeat if you wish to. People who suffer from backache should repeat this Asana as required and hold for a longer period.

25. This Asana is similar to No. 22 with a slight variation.

A. Lying on your back bring your feet towards your bottom and then bend your knees towards the right so that the right knee touches the ground and the left leg rests on the right leg. Then lift the right leg and put it on top of the left knee and press it to touch the ground. While the arms are stretched up towards the left side of the head and the head turned to look at the hands. Legs bent towards the right and arms stretched up towards the left. Hold for a while in this stretched position and then slowly release to lie straight. Normalize breathing.

B. Repeat this by bending the knees towards the left and then bring the left knee on top of the right knee while the body and the arms are stretched out towards the right, arms beyond the head and the eyes looking at the stretched hands. Hold for a while and then release the posture and slowly return to lying down straight. Then inhale and exhale. Better repeat the entire Assan on both the sides and then perform Shav Assan to normalize breathing.

26. Attempt this Asana a few weeks after beginning when the body stiffness has reduced. Lying flat on the floor, bend both the elbows backwards and place the palms below the shoulder, fingers pointing towards the feet.

B. Bring your feet nearest to your bottom about 4 inches apart. Then slowly lift your hips, back and chest up with the support of the feet, the palms and the stretched arms as the back curves like a bow, hold for a comfortable while. Then slowly bring your hips and back down to touch the ground. Then straighten your legs and bring your hands back next to the body. Perform Shav Assan to normalize breathing.

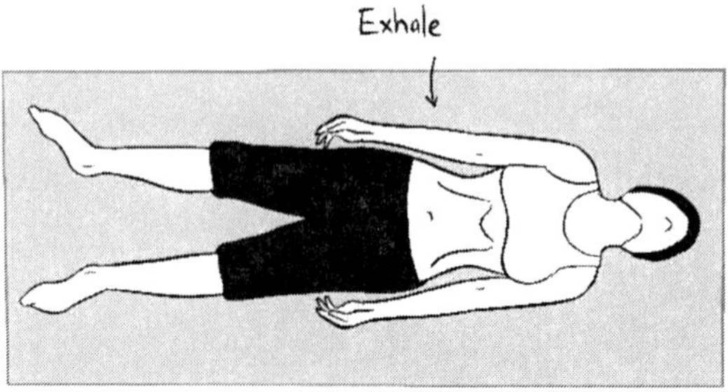

27. Lying down inhale slowly and deeply, exhale slowly, deeply and completely, and ensure no air is left in the lungs or the stomach and then pull your stomach in as much as possible; hold your breath in this state as long as possible and then very slowly start inhaling and fill the lungs. Repeat this once. This is a very beneficial Asana, the entire abdomen gets exercised and holding the breath out also strengthens the lungs.

28. Slowly sit up, arms by the side, take the support of your elbows in the beginning if necessary, and sit cross legged inhale and exhale. Hold your hands behind your back, inhale and while exhaling, bend your head in front towards the ground and lift your hands straight up behind the back towards the head and hold for a while. Keep breathing, then bring your head towards your right knee and try to touch your head with it, hold for a while. Then bring your head towards the left knee and try to touch the head with the knee and hold for a while. Then bring the head back towards the middle and

release your arms, bring them in front and rest the hands on your knees. Inhale and exhale slowly and deeply until breathing normalizes. Repeat the Assan.

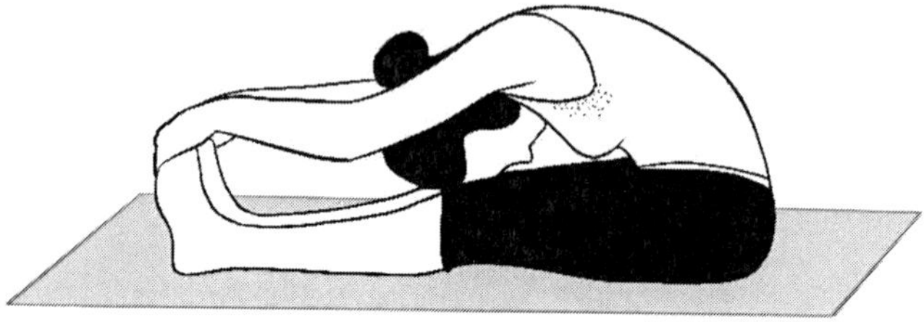

29. While sitting, stretch the legs in front, raise your hands above the head, arms stretched up, and then bring the hands down to catch the toes; if not possible in the beginning, bring the hands nearest to the feet. Then bring the head towards the knees, clasp it with your hands and gently press the head towards the knees and try to touch the head on the knees or hold as near as possible, for a comfortable while. Release and straighten the back and bring the arms to your sides, inhale and exhale, and lie down slowly, don't drop, and normalize breathing.

30. A. Sit up slowly and spread the straight legs apart so that the feet are as far apart from each other as comfortable.

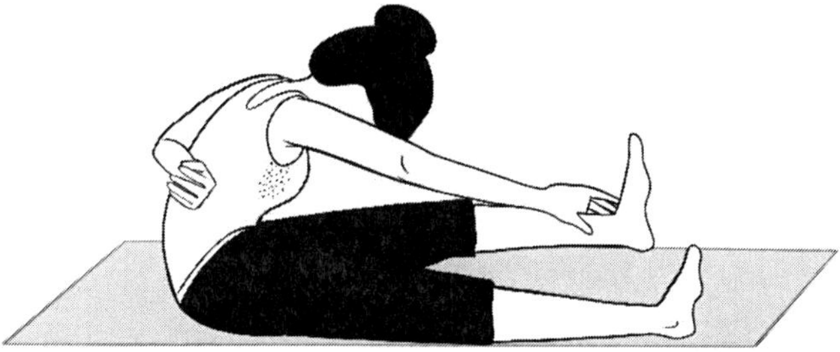

B. Then bend forward and try to catch the left side of your left foot with your right hand or hold your hand as near to the left foot as possible. Meanwhile, curve the left arm behind your back and bring your head towards the left knee and try to touch it, hold for a while and then slowly return to sitting straight while the legs remain spread. Now try to catch your right foot with your left hand, or hold it as near as possible. Meanwhile twist your right arm behind your back and bring the head as close as possible to the right knee. Hold for a comfortable while and release the posture; bring your feet together inhale and exhale and repeat the Assan. Then join your legs, sit cross legged and perform Pranayam to normalize breathing.

31. This Asana may be difficult to perform in the beginning but it is a very important one and you should attempt it

when the stiffness in the body has reduced, after a few weeks of yoga practice.

A. While sitting, fold your left knee and bring the heel close to your bottom, then lift the right foot and place it behind the left knee.

B. Now, bring your left arm behind the right knee and try to hold right foot with your left hand or hold the hand as near as possible to the right foot.

C. While the right arm goes behind the back and the head turned towards the right and the torso also twists towards the right. Hold for a comfortable while and keep breathing. Then slowly release the twists and stretch your leg out.

D. Now fold the right leg and bring it close to the bottom, lift the left foot and place it behind the right knee. Then bring the right arm behind the left knee and try to hold the left foot or get your hand as close to it as possible. Meanwhile the left arm goes behind the back along with the torso twisting towards the left and the head twisting towards the left as far as possible. Hold as long as is comfortable and then release and sit cross legged and perform Pranayam to normalize breathing. Then stretch your legs in front and lie down slowly, without the aid of your hands. Normalize breathing, if need be.

32. A. Now turn and lie on your stomach. Fold your arms under your head and rest one side of the face on the arms keeping breathing. Slowly lift your head, shoulders and chest, while straightening the arms completely and bending the head backwards

along with the waist bending backwards and forming a small curve. Hold for a comfortable while.

B. Then turn your head towards the left and try to look at the right heel and hold and then turn your head towards the right and try to look at your left heel and hold and then straighten the head. Slowly bring your head and chest down along with the arms, fold them in front and rest one side of your face on your folded arms. Inhale and exhale and normalize breathing. Repeat the Assan once or twice.

33. Lying on the stomach with the arms and the hands next to your body with palms facing upwards and chin on the ground, lift your left leg up backward towards your head, keep it straight and hold for a while, then slowly bring it down and breathe normally. Now lift the right leg backward up towards your head, hold for a while, and then bring it down slowly, without bending it. Fold

your arms in front and rest your face on your hands and inhale and exhale to normalize breathing. Repeat once or twice.

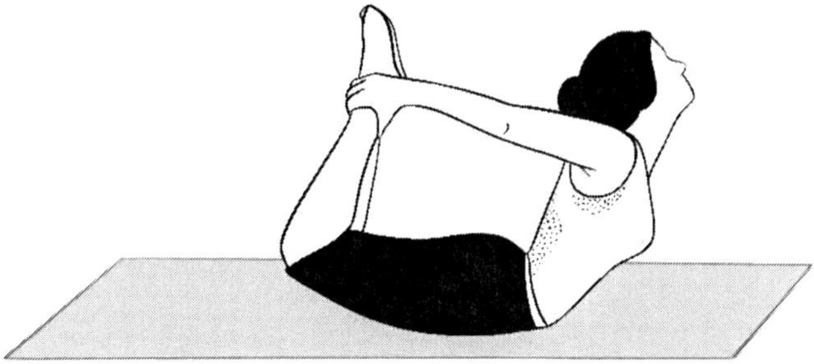

34. Lying on the stomach, bend both knees inwards keeping the heels about 4 inches apart above your buttocks. Firmly catch hold of your ankles with your hands and then slowly lift up your chest with the head bending backward and the feet pushing out, and the back curved like a bow. Hold as far as possible and then slowly release your legs and bring your arms to the side. Fold your arms in front, rest your face on your hands and normalize breathing. Repeat if you want to.

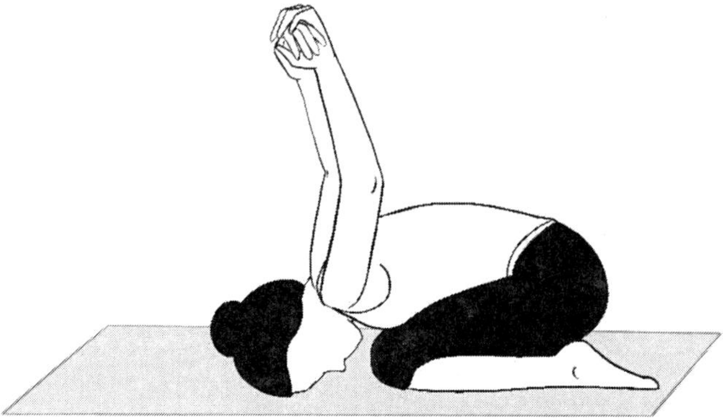

35. A. Lift the chest with the help of your arms and hands and sit on your folded legs and then inhale and exhale. Hold your hands behind your back and bend forward and bring your head down to touch the ground in front of your knees, while the held hands go up towards your head and hold for a while.

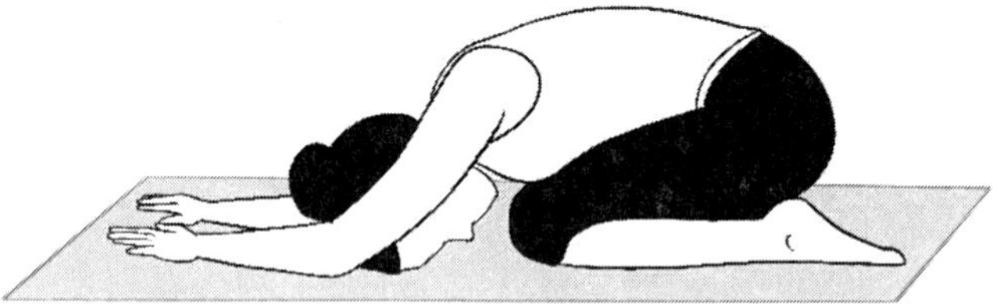

B. Then release the hands and stretch your arms in front as far as possible, while the head remains touching the ground. Hold for a while and then slowly return to sitting cross-legged and perform Pranayam.

36. Push-Ups. Once again lie on your stomach and bring your palms next to the shoulder with the feet fingers on the ground and lift your body up straight and then bring it down slowly. Repeat this five times. Then turn to lie on your back and Perform Shav Asana (20) and, if need be, perform Pranayam to normalize breathing.

37. A. Stand up erect, face, and mind calm heels about to 6 to 8 inches apart and keep your hands on the waist and bend forward so that your chest is parallel to the ground. Start rotating at the waist towards the right and continue to rotate backward so that the back comes parallel to the ground below, while the face is looking up. Hold for a second or two and then continue to complete the rotating circle towards the left and bringing the torso towards the front and hold the chest parallel to the ground below for a while and keep breathing.

    B. Now repeat this by rotation to towards the left and completing the circle. When the rotation is complete straighten up and perform Pranayam. Repeat the entire Asana if you wish.

38. Stand erect, with heels about 9 to 12inches apart as comfortable and then bend forward about 45 degrees and hold your thighs, with your spread fingers above the knees. Then inhale and exhale slowly and completely so that no air is left in the lungs. Now, pull the abdomen in as much as possible and hold your breath, then start rotating the abdomen along with your hips; continue as far as is comfortable. Stop the rotation and, while still

bent, inhale slowly. Then, while exhaling, lift your chest and return to a normal standing posture, inhale and exhale and perform Pranayam. Gradually increase the stomach rotation time, as this Assan leads to the exercise of the entire organs in the abdomen. It becomes easy with practice and is very effective.

39. Stand erect, open your eyes wide along with the mouth and then stick your tongue out as much as possible and hold in this position for a while, then relax the face and repeat the action twice or more.

40. Stand erect, open your eyes wide and look up, hold for a second or two then look down; after a second or two close your eyes. Open the eyes, head straight, and look towards the right and hold, and then look towards the left and hold, and then close the eyes. Open again and look to the upper left side of the eye, hold and then look towards the lower right side and hold. Now look to the upper right side and hold, then look to the lower left side, and then close the eyes. Open and slowly rotate them in a clockwise direction, at first lookup, then to the right, and then down and finally to the left. Repeat anti-clockwise, before closing the eyes. Open the eyes and raise one arm and stretch it in front of the eyes, close your fist, raise the forefinger and bring it to eye level. Then focus the eyes on the fingertip and bring it slowly towards the nose, and then straighten the arm while the eyes remain fixed on the fingertip, then bring your hand down and close the eyes. Rub your hands firmly until they are warm. Then cup your hands over the closed eyes and let the warmth and darkness relax them.

This is the end of the yoga session: The body and the mind are relaxed and harmonized, as an internal bath has taken place. With the regular practice of yoga, body metabolism improves along with immunity. There is the feeling of well-being, and of being healthy, and you are energized and ready to take on the world, with the intake of proper food.

One Assan with which reducesfatigue to a great extent, after a long and hard day, is as follows:

41. This Assan may be difficult for some in the beginning but with practice, it becomes easy and, no matter how tired one feels, with this Assan fatigue will almost vanish.

A. Sit on the ground, lift your left foot and place it on the right thigh, then lift your right foot and place it on the left thigh. Keep your Hands-on your knees, thumb and for fingerheld in a circle and arms rest stretched out. Sit in this manner, as far as comfortable.In the beginning, it could be half a minute but with time it can be as long as you require, depending upon how tired you are. Unwind the legs and now repeat this Assan in reverse.

B. Now, lift the right foot and place it on the left thigh and then lift the left foot and place it on the right thigh. Sit in this manner as long as comfortable to get rid of the fatigue in the legs.

Though a proper yoga session in the morning with some exercise is enough to live a healthy life another session in the evening, when the stomach is empty, without emphasis on deep breathing, as the air is not fresh then, would lead to a relaxed body, calmer mind, better appetite, and hence better sleep. It's a win-win situation.

42. One last unique, simple, and effective exercise for the entire family. Place two chairs in a room about 6 feet apart, if necessary less and an hour before going to sleep. And walk in formation 8 around and between these chairs for about 20 minutes, at a pace you prefer. Once again don't let the mind wander or chatter instead keep it silent. Or start chanting as explained hereafter in this Book. The benefits of this exercise are great though silent. People with morbidities benefit no less if not more, than the healthy and the elderly.

Yoga is generally thought to be a physical activity but it started as a mental exercise known as Raj Yog later corrupted as Yoga, the physical part is known as Hath Yog. It could be stated that Hath Yog developed to assist Raj Yog. After the practice of Hath Yog, which leads to relaxing the body and mind the practice of Raj Yog, described as Meditation in English, becomes easier. The benefits of meditation are known to all and meditation will assist to combat corona. Why not, a stable and calm mind always carries one well in life in all respects, and with meditation, fear should have no space in the mind. Hath Yoga and Raj Yoga combined would beat this scourge better. When one is physically and mentally strong, success comes along.

Under present circumstances and even otherwise, time is there as long as one realizes the importance of the undertaking. If one is unable to find time for one's wellbeing then can one, live a meaningful life? One can only help others when one is strong himself or herself.

After the physical yoga session is over, it is time to practice mental yoga, and one of the suitable times is immediately after the Yoga session is over in the morning, though a sitting in the evening after a Yoga session or before sleeping can enhance its effects. Meditation can elevate the mind to a state of tranquility, serenity, and joy, and this can take place if one practices meditation regularly and with determination. It is a process whereby a word or a sentence is chanted to stop the constant churning of the mind. In other words make it rest or become silent, which leads to its tranquility.

Any sentence or a word that appeals to oneself can be chanted. One word, which is unique because it contains all the vowels, A E I O U & M pronounced as AUM, has been found to be effective. Why? Because like vowels, it is produced when the breath flows through the mouth without being blocked by the teeth, tongue or lips. The M at the end completes the word. When the seven colors of the spectrum are rotated, the result is white and if A E I O U M were to be rotated as a spectrum, then the sound will be Ohm, it has a scientific base. Though no meanings can be assigned to it, the word 'peace' appears to be the most suitable.

This is the word or the sound used by Professor Henry Higgins when he takes up the challenge to perfect the pronunciation of Eliza Doolittle to enable her to talk in refined English and behave like a lady, If you can, read the book or watch the film 'My fair lady'

As mentioned earlier, any word or a sentence which appeals to oneself can be chanted. People who believe in a Supreme Power can use the name different religion assigns to it like Elohim, God, Allah, Ohm Namo Shiva, Sat Nam Shree Whey Guru. It is to be noted by those who believe in the Supreme Power that it never named itself, it is humans who have named it and then fight and kill each other over it.

However, chant the word or name which appeals to you. Sit cross-legged, on the floor or a hard bed, absolutely erect, and hold the head high. Rest your hand on the knees, join the thumbs and forefingers, stretch the other three fingers in front and breathe normally. If sitting cross-legged is not comfortable in the beginning, eventually one gets used to it. It is better to develop this habit, as it is the healthiest posture for sitting and aids meditation. Otherwise, sit straight on the edge of a chair when the feet can rest on the floor and the legs remain straight. Imagine aunflickering candle flame burning in the middle of your eyebrows. Focus your mind on it and start chanting the word of choice, or any of the sentences known as 'mantras' mentioned below. The mind may start to wander; if so, bring it back gently. In the beginning, the mind continues to wander repeatedly, do not struggle with it, and continue to bring it back gently to focusing it on the candlelight. Another way to discipline the mind is to challenge it to go ahead and wander, and it stops naturally after a while.

Eventually, the mind starts to wander less and less, and a time will come when it will wander no more for a short period in the beginning, which increases with time. This is when you start feeling peaceful and a time comes when one does not want to stop meditating. And eventually, the sense of time and space is lost and one starts to enjoy the serenity or tranquility of the mind. With continuous practice, one day the mind achieves a state of joy, which can be experienced but cannot be described – provided there is the desire to achieve this state. And, to achieve such a state, one's way of life has to be simple and not involved in conflicts, which arise owing to ego or selfishness or other negative attributes one may be living with. In short, live a life of truthfulness or righteousness to be able to achieve a higher state of the mind where joy prevails.

Meditation can take place anytime, anywhere the least it can achieve is to reduce stress; say while stuck in a travel jam, waiting for anunknown period for whatever purpose. Or traveling for long, or when there is nothing else to do and the mind starts to get agitated or is bored or distressed, start meditating and feel the good change.

Single-word chanting is suitable for some minds but others may prefer chanting a phrasal mantra; following are some suggestions:-

Sarve bhavantu sukhinah
(May all become happy)

Sarve santu niramayah.
(May all be free from illness)

Sarve bhadrani pashyantu.
(May all know the truth)

Makaschit dukb bhagbhawe.
(May no one suffers)

A simple and effective Tibetan Buddhist Mantra.

Ohm Mani Padme Hum.

Ohm Mani Padme Hum.

Ohm praise, to the Jewel in the Lotus.

A Muslim prayer.

LA ILAHA ILLALLAH Muhammad ur Rasulullah. There is no God but one 'Allah'. Mohammed is his Prophet.

If Muslims, do not wish to focus their minds on the candle, then they could sit facing the Kaaba and fix their mind it on it and chant the Kalima.

Also, instead of chanting the Kalima, they could just chant the name of Allah which would lead to the tranquility of the mind, provided the mind is not allowed to wander and remains fixed.

Children should be encouraged to chant a mantra aloud, if possible, in a group. It leads to a relaxed and calm mind.

One can chant any mantra, which appeals to the mind, but it ought to be rhythmical, but a mantra should be chanted and not sung.

It is claimed that it is better not to know the meaning of the mantra as it could distract the mind. Also chanting a mantra in a language other than the mother tongue is more effective. Chant any name or any mantra with dedication and belief the result is the same, provided it takes place with regularity and with the required simple mindset, as mentioned above, to achieve the goal of meditation; that of a harmonious, tranquil and alleviated state of mind, where joy prevails, and one's true nature is revealed. Constant practice and the sincere intense desire and longing for the state of joy will be achieved provided a life of righteousness and compassion is lived.

Developing of immunity is required by people in all walks of life, including children going to school. Students going to the universities, teachers and all other staff working in the universities, workers in industrial plants, at construction sites, people working in government and private offices, shops, restaurants, and most of all people working in hospitals and clinics including Doctors. Police personnel are being stuck by this scourge and need to be prepared. In fact, the entire working population of this world has to get back to work for this world to stand on its feet as before. Developing immunity and basic health is the answer, without any fear in the mind.

Besides Yoga and exercise whenever there is an opportunity walk, including up the stairs instead of using lifts. In the beginning, it could be just one or two floors, and getting used to walking up several floors by middle-aged people is not difficult if there is the will to do so. The young should run up the stairs instead of walking at a quick pace. Don't use the escalators at the Metros, or other places, instead walk or run up the stairs.

Elderly people who have locked themselves in their homes and have not exercised and their diet has not been under control, would probably end up with diabetes or other health problems. Besides starting with exercise, they should move out of the house and get to a place where they can breathe fresh air and walk around especially in the mornings. But, keep their nose and mouth covered, if they are walking in places with people around and get to an open space before they can remove the mask to breathe fresh air, where nobody is around in the vicinity of two meters or more.

Smokers who are in the danger zone ought to give up smoking and it can be achieved by beginning to exercise as suggested and reducing the number of cigarettes smoked gradually. Suppose this number is a packet of 20 cigarettes a day, take out4 cigarettes from the packet and keep them aside, the next day take out 5 and keep it aside. On the third day keep out 6 and keep them aside. Forth day do not buy any cigarettes and smoke the 13 out of the 15 you have saved. After this reduce a cigarette every day or reduce one every other day. Rest depends on your will power and it is not difficult to give it up entire unless you have been smoking for decades. In which case reduce them to three a day.

Appetite will improve with reduced smoking and so would your health. Besides, you arc not harming family and friends any more owing to passive smoking. And you are saving money for a good purpose. It's a win-win situation.

Before suggestions are made for a healthy diet for grownups, one important suggestion is never to overeat. It is better to eat about 10% less than one's appetite while taking breakfast and about 15% less when taking lunch and 20% less when taking dinner. This does not mean one is eating about 40% less in a day that would be disastrous. Whatever is eaten less during one meal it is covered during the next. This method just helps the digestive system to work without strain and digest food better and remain healthy, it ends up living longer.

Generally, our intake of cereals like wheat and rice is more than required, so eat less of these and more of the other good foods, like vegetables, fruits, nuts, and even more of those which provide protein like eggs, poultry, and fish. Another good source of protein is lintels and beans which also contain fiber.

Every hour and before meals, drink a glass of water except when other liquids have been consumed.

To reiterate, the following suggestions are for 5 days in a week; the other two days eat what you like, but not oil-rich food.

About 20 minutes after your yoga session is over, mix in a large glass, three forth of a teaspoon of each of turmeric powder, dry ginger powder, flake seed powder, and black pepper. Besides less than half a teaspoon of black sesame powder and black onion seeds powder (also known as black caraway seeds). Pour hot water after boiling and brew for about two minutes then keep stirring and drinking it slowly. If you find it strong and difficult to drink then add some honey and lemon.

Take it for five days a week and you may not start until the middle age unless you are basically weak.

Properties: of the ingredients of the drink.

Turmeric Powder: Potent anti-inflammatory and antioxidant. Has the potential to prevent heart diseases and arthritis. Probably may help, to prevent cancer and Alzheimer

Dry Ginger powder: Helps digestion, burns fat, helps maintain cholesterol and blood sugar level, and reduces pain.

Flake seeds powder: Loaded with nutrients, high in Omega 3 fats, rich in dietary fiber. Also, a rich source of Lignans, which may reduce cancer risk.

Black Pepper powder: High in antioxidants and boosts absorption of nutrients. May improve brain and gut health.

Black Sesame Powder: rich in Vitamin B, Iron, and anti-aging properties.

Black Onion Seeds Powder: Helps control diabetes and blood pressure, Protects kidney, and may help assist asthma patients.

Alternative drink. Honey in hot water with lemon, diabetics should consult their Doctors before taking honey with this drink.

Breakfast: Should be the healthiest meal. All meals chew well and don't eat in a hurry. Eating the right food, in the right way, at the right time and the right quantity can make or break your health. Some people are in the habit of not taking proper breakfast and this should change. Eat early at night and eat more fibrous food to be able to clear your stomach in the morning.

Start breakfast with fruits: an apple, an orange or a grapefruit. For a change or addition, it could a cup of pomegranate. Weight watchers eat as much fruit as you can.

Wash and soak in water overnight about eight almonds and two walnuts. Wash and soak 3 or 4 dried figs for a few minutes before breakfast which can be taken along with the walnuts. Also, take about 2 or 3 dates at the end of the meal. (Diabetics should avoid figs and dates).

For working and young, take two half-boiled eggs (because they are easiest to digest) or one half-boiled and one three-quarters boiled egg for the sake of taste. For a change, you can take poached eggs. Also, take only the white portion of one boiled egg. Depending upon your profession, age, and body structure, and your body requirement, you could take half the yolk or the entire yolk of the boiled egg. Elderly people or those with less appetite can reduce the intake of the half-boiled eggs to one a day. Besides salt, eggs, especially boiled, should be taken with plenty of lemons, not only for taste but to add Vitamin C to them, which they lack.It was once said 'An apple a day, keeps the doctor away'; now, 'An apple, an orange plus two eggs a day, keeps the doctor away'.

Then preferably take a bowl of oatmeal made with some amount of low-fat milk and a banana, for change take muesli with low-fat milk and a banana. Greek yogurt is the recommended addition. Heavy eaters could also add brown bread and cheese but no butter. The total intake depends upon individual requirement; one should not be left hungry, or ever over-eat, which does not leave you fighting fit for the day ahead.

The recommended beverage is coffee or green tea without milk or sugar. Those who are used to taking white coffee or tea could do so but cut the sugar, which is now considered slow poisoning as it increases the risk of dementia and probably even cancer and Alzheimer's.

Lunch should be light but nutritious as not to feel lethargic and, instead, remain alert and active.

A glass of fresh juice would be ideal, to begin with. Or any other preferred drink, but no colas. The ideal beverage, water, is always there if there is no desire for any other drink. Next, a bowl of salad is a good choice, with as many raw edible vegetables, herbs, and seeds as possible. The ingredients could change from time to time for taste and convenience; in fact, eating different kinds of ingredients is better; portions of each can be small if the ingredients are many.

Those who have a better appetite add a piece of bread and or cheese. Simple dressings, such as salt and fresh lemon or just plain yogurt, or vinegar with olive or salad oil are good. For a change, take any dressing but avoid heavy dressings.

Addition of cottage cheese or a boiled egg, add to the variety in salads which can be vast, but the basic ingredients should be raw vegetables, herbs, and seeds. When there is appetite and for a change, have a potato and egg salad.

Another suggestion is to take a simple brown bread sandwich, if possible, of fresh cottage cheese with fresh mint leaf along with an apple or pear or both or a glass of juice. The other option is of brown bread with cucumber and tomato without butter with an apple or pear, or both, or a glass of juice.

Other lighter meal suggestions: Banana milkshake. Yogurt and fruits mixed. Just a bowl of yogurt or buttermilk if there is no appetite. These are just suggestions; the aim is to have a light meal for lunch, the choice is yours, eat whatever is convenient and whatever you like, but about 15% short of a full stomach. A hot beverage after any meal helps digestion and a glass of hot water is probably easiest to take and good as well. A cold drink or a glass of cold water after meals hinders digestion.

It is necessary to consume water throughout the day or occasionally take other beverages; good options are green, mint, or cinnamon tea or black coffee all without milk or sugar. Fresh fruit juice or mixed fruit and vegetable juice, such as carrot and orange or carrot and beetroot. Salted lemonade or any other drink you like with the least possible amount of sugar better none at all, but colas, as infrequently as possible, better none at all.

Snacks: black chocolate, dried and fresh berries especially blueberries, fresh and dried fruits, including dry apricots, dry figs, and dates, preferably those not consumed in the morning. Nuts, seeds, and chickpeas/hummus. Better to not eat biscuits. Potato Chips and other such fried snacks, along with sweets, are the worst to take.

Dinner: If you have not had a bowl of salad in the afternoon, then a bowl before dinner should be a must. Even if you have had a salad in the afternoon, a small bowl is suggested. Besides the usual tomatoes, onions, cucumber, lettuce, and cabbage, a good salad, if possible, should contain some of these vegetables: asparagus, broccoli, red bell peppers, cauliflower, radish, artichoke, celery, spring onions, red cabbage, beetroot and not to be left out is garlic and ginger, herbs like coriander, mint, oregano, and peppermint should be added to the salad. Seeds add to salad's value and should be used when possible, such as pumpkin, chia, and hemp. Garlic and Ginger have optimum food value and should be taken raw daily in salads or otherwise. Sprouts another important intake can be mixed with the salad or taken separately.

Then eat what you like; different kinds of foods, Chinese, Indian, French, Japanese, and food from other parts of the world, but cooked with care and love, and not in a hurried manner. Eat more of dark-colored and leafy vegetables, such as spinach, red leaf lettuce, kale, red/purple cabbage, romaine lettuce, purple sweet potato, eggplant, Chinese long beans, purple turnips, beets, purple okra. Beans and lentils should also be part of your regular diet, especially for vegetarians, for the necessary intake of protein. Beans or lentils are essential when non-vegetarian food is not being taken.

Amongst the non-vegetarian foods, fish is rated at the top for low-fat protein, and also other types of seafood have great value in terms of protein content. Shrimps, crab, lobster, scallops, oysters, prawns, squid, mussels, crawfish, and cuttlefish, though costing more than other types of food, can be taken whenever possible, especially since there is low-fat content in most seafood. Next, good meats are poultry, basically chicken, turkey, and quails. Finally, the red meats of goats and sheep are safer to take if these animals are grazed and not produced at a farm. Red meat, if cooked properly, is highly nutritious, loaded with healthy protein, healthy fats, vitamins, and minerals, especially iron and Vitamin B12 which is good for the brain besides it has various other nutrients. People who exercise and growing children should be taking red meat for overall good health and to beat Covid-19 but in moderation and take beans and lintels as well.

A small amount of dessert is fine but the best dessert to take is fruits such as sweet melon, mango, pears, plums, grapes, peaches, papaya, apricots, and watermelon, all ripe and sweet. It is better to take two of them after dinner. These fruits help digestion and reduce constipation. A cup of yogurt, especially sour, after food, helps digestion. Another good intake after dinner is Jaggery. It is loaded with antioxidants and minerals, including zinc and selenium, which help prevent free-radicals, responsible for early aging. It is said to help buildimmunity as well.

On the other two days eat more or less what you like, but avoid deep-fried foods and foods which contain refined wheat flour. Take your dinner at least two hours before sleep, if not more, so that you can sleep well and live long.

Diet chart for the overweight:

Breakfast-

Take an Apple and an Orange. Soak about 8 almonds and two walnuts in water overnight, peel, and eat in the morning. Take one half-boiled egg and white of 2 to 8 eggs, as per your age, weight, and the desire to lose weight. Also, if need be, can take a very small quantity of Muesli with some low-fat milk. Or small quantity of Corn Flakes with low-fat milk can also be taken. Take a large glass of Green Tea or black coffee. In the case of white tea/coffee take no sugar. Never forget, each meal eat 20% less than a full stomach.

Beverage: A glass of hot water every hour.

Lunch: Only Salad with seeds and a simple dressing of lemon with the least bit of salt or low-fat Yogurt. Sometimes use oil and vinegar.

Snacks: If need be, a carrot, cucumber, tomato, or lettuce leaves.

Dinner: Different types of soup which could include a light soup made from beans and lentils. Take some more salad and or sprouts. Steamed or boiled vegetables, steamed fish, or some boiled poultry. Take enough fruits like mango, sweet melon, peaches, and plums; the fruits taken should be not less than 20% of the meal.

Twice a week, only for dinner, you can have the food you like, with the least bit of oil. Be sure not to remain constipated. Walk for half an hour in the 8 formations after dinner, besides, Yoga and other exercises.

Diet, for very heavy people, under the guidance of a Doctor.

Just stop eating completely and drink hot water throughout the day and take a Multivitamin/Multi mineral Pill.

The only other intake allowed is coconut water once a day.

Initially, hunger pangs will be there but will power has to be there. Eventually, the fat in the body starts melting and the weight starts to reduce.

A minimum of seven days at a stretch is necessary but more the better if you can and your doctor allows you to continue.

The first meal should be a small glass of fresh juice and then just fruits and yogurt for three days after which eat only raw food for as many days as possible or necessary. Which could include raw vegetables, nuts, seeds, sprouts, but no cooked food. When the required weight loss has taken place, start with taking soups and some bread and eat light for another few days. After this, decide what to eat bearing in mind suggestions made in this book. But never forget to eat 20% less of every meal.

Known bad habits.

1. Missing breakfast.
2. Sleeping late
3. High sugar consumption
4. Oversleeping or not sleeping enough.
5. Eating meals while watching TV/Computer.
6. Not drinking enough water.
7. A habit of holding urine.

With improved health and immunity, owing to the healthy lifestyle of regular exercise, proper diet, proper sleep, proper mental attitude, and the required precautions there should be no fear of any virus.

The world has to move on and everyone should start working, except the elderly, and living their normal happy life as before. Including, going out for shopping, buying cars and other goods, eating in restaurants, and those who can afford to take holidays.

If this does not take place the world economic situation could deteriorate further and human suffering could increase to unimaginable heights.

"Yoga exercises strengthen the respiratory system, the digestive system, and the blood purification and circulation system. Along with other exercises and a proper diet, one can obtain high levels of immunity. This will not only prepare one to combat and overcome any virus or bacterial attack better, but it would also lead to the prevention of diabetes, hypertension and would keep cardiovascular attacks at bay. It's a win-win situation."

"If you find this Book worth a read and you feel it could benefit your friends, family and colleagues, then please inform them about this Book. In this manner you will also help complete education of a poor child."

Youtube Video Links For Reference

- https://studio.youtube.com/video/091JTfzZq9I/edit/basic exercises 1to 7
- https://studio.youtube.com/video/_A67M2jZ9Qc/edit/basic 8 to 11
- https://studio.youtube.com/video/c9h9xtn7X8Y/edit/basic 12 to 18
- https://studio.youtube.com/video/QCaJAG4x0Iw/edit/basic 19 to 23
- https://studio.youtube.com/video/_iUBEDOnH3I/edit/basic 24,25,26
- https://studio.youtube.com/video/6Ooc89xSa-k/edit/basic 31 and 36
- https://studio.youtube.com/video/AfmY3MNGEpI/edit/basic 32 to 35, 41